BOOKS BY PETER DAVISON

POETRY

MEMOIR

CRITICISM

EDITOR

BREATHING ROOM

BREATHING ROOM

New Poems

PETER DAVISON

Alfred A. Knopf   New York   2002

THIS IS A BORZOI BOOK
PUBLISHED BY ALFRED A. KNOPF

www.randomhouse.com/knopf/poetry

Some of these poems have been published in *The Atlantic Monthly,* the *Boston Globe,*
Country Journal, DoubleTake, Five Points, The Georgia Review,
Michigan Quarterly Review, The Nation, The New Republic, Orion, The Paris Review,
Partisan Review, Poetry, Stand, and *The Yale Review* (details on page 65).
I am grateful to the editors of those periodicals for printing the individual poems,
and to the Corporation of Yaddo, the Bellagio Study Center, and the Fondazione Bogliasco
for generous support during this book's composition.

Library of Congress Cataloging-in-Publication Data
Davison, Peter.
Breathing room : new poems / Peter Davison.
p.   cm.
ISBN 0-375-70937-1
I. Title.
PS3554.A94 B77 2000
811'.54—dc21   00-023277

Manufactured in the United States of America
Published September 26, 2000
First Paperback Edition Published April 9, 2002

FOR JOAN

COMPLETELY

CONTENTS

CATCHES OF BREATH: A Foreword

The poems in *Breathing Room* mostly assume a single poetic form. I was tempted to call them "audiographs," since, like photographs, each is of a particular dimension and utilizes the same aesthetic, what Robert Pinsky calls the "technology of the breath." Each is intended to evoke a mood, a scene, an enigma, the unfolding of a metaphor, the entrapment of an idea, in a space or shape that will contain it without killing it. Poetry composes, not as modern Western music often does, for an instrument or for an orchestra or recording device, but for the human breath. The breath is the most intimate aspect of our existence. It connects us to the biosphere. Breath makes our voice operate. It enables oxygen to penetrate our bodies. Breath lends us rhyme and meter, the means by which poetry came into existence. Time may be able to teach us new ways of using our minds, but I very much doubt whether it can teach us anything new about ways of breathing—or even about what happens to our being when we can no longer breathe. Poetry began, I think, as a mnemonic device to enable an illiterate populace to remember prayers, to recite the order of worship, or, in a more secular use, to recount the inventories of warehouses in ancient Babylon. That's why we wrote in rhyme and meter, so that we could remember what we thought we had compiled; hence the connection of words to breath to sense to mind to memory to rhythm to emotion to memory.

The past is where we are from. It is what we are most of. To remember is to keep things that have already happened from sliding into oblivion. Poets have more to learn from the past than they will ever understand, but the best way to learn poetry is to learn it by heart. To learn poetry we need to take poems into our breath and blood, and that requires us to hear them as we read them, to learn to read with all the senses, especially with the ear. If we learn techniques for understanding poetry, no harm is done; but there can be no substitute for learning poetry itself. We need to meet the art on its own ground; we need to hold poetry in the ear, by the hand, in the head. The more poetry I contain in my head, the more of poetry I may comprehend, for I will find myself breathing in the very impulse. When I've learned a poem by heart (lovely phrase), I shall have read it completely, with all I can bring to it, and I shall own something that will still be mine in bankruptcy, in prison, or on my deathbed. My challenge as a poet is to write poems well enough so that other people will desire to learn them—so as to entertain themselves under every circumstance.

So, are these poems audiographs? I think not. Catches of breath, maybe. And the book gives them room enough to lie down in.

Peter Davison
December 1999

SPELL AT A STUDIO IN ITALY

Blessèd little house,
give my verse a chance
herein to arouse,
shake itself, and dance.

Others here have pressed
brain to burst its bonds,
mind to do its best,
soul to make amends.

You who follow us,
know that for a while
Como hallowed us.
Change. Write. Smile.

I

Thou Hast nor Youth . . .

NO ESCAPE

No, not yet, move nothing until
    you have filled yourself with
        intention, or

your act will freeze, immutable, and
    your thought will have aborted
        into misshapen stumbling.

We stammer in the effort to speak, lurch
    out of a passion to walk, slump
        in lieu of sitting; yet,

within, awareness may reach toward
    an attainable state in which
        we seek to direct our selves

as a rider guides the most accomplished of
    horses, crupper gathering, hooves
        pattering, neck yearning toward

heaven, the supple trunk conveying
    itself over the earth without
        anticipation or effort.

This is the ascent into the self,
    encountering possibility just as it
        flowers into the actual.

We attain fulfilment only if we carry
    the breath of the world
        without surrender
        or escape.

CONFEDERATES

My dear sidekick, though you've kept me company
       ever since adolescence, I've never yet
              seen so much as a fleck of dandruff

on your blue suit. While I squinted for the wingbeat
       of a bird, you priced the binoculars.
              As I trudged, lame-ankled, along the upland path,

you reminded me we were due at work, where
       I tapped out desk-memos while you
              made plans for lunch.

In the hot toils of lust, there you stood,
       reckoning how much it would cost to pay for
              a second sweet night in this fleabag, and

when it came to romance, I sat on moss
       by a pond, the edgy hand of a redhaired girl
              in mine, and caught you calculating

whether life with her might not be
       very convenient, considering her parents'
              money. And when, at last,

I found requited passion, who but you
       warned me we would never be able to afford
              the expense of our beloved's divorce?

Bar sinister! Not a friend, but not qualified as
       an enemy: you can't look me in the eye, can you?
              Can't face up after
              all these years in lockstep?

4

Which of us Kept In Touch?
      You, with your warnings of anxiety and dread,
        your greeds and grudges, or

I, numerical idiot, mooning over
      alternatives, friendships, despising whatever
        arrangement looked feasible, attempting

to ignore your hard questions and stacking of
      the odds? I, headless horseman, was impelled to
        plunge in after a drowning child. You

asked *why*. I thirsted to risk all
      at play, on stage, in love or aloud. You
        counselled profit-taking, tact, concessions

and budgets. I had the instinct
      to give it all away. You advised
        saving that till later. And didn't you in fact

rescue us so that we stayed afloat together
      downstream, drifting quietly past
        a thousand alternatives we had luckily abandoned,

including my doomed quest to explore
      the country on the far side?
        So now we fetch up, unchallenged,

on the coast of a middle-aged moderate clime, cautiously
      tucked in the world's pocket.
        You have never forgiven me.
        I have never forgiven you.

DUST BOWL

Our new blue 1934 Chevrolet found
        its voice while following concrete guidelines
                from Captiva toward Tallahassee,

Mobile, Shreveport, and Fort Worth.
        Everything our future called for was stowed
                in the trunk. After Wichita the sky

began to darken. The Chevrolet's noise
        darkened too, responding to
                something in the air. My father

gunned the engine to clear
        the car's throat, while my mother redressed grievances
                and settled counterclaims filed from

the children's outback behind the driver's seat.
        East of Dodge City the sky clamped down,
                the car took to muttering, and we

broke the trip in a nearly empty hotel
        where the windows leaked brown powder and
                our feet scraped on the bathroom tiles.

Grit gathered on our teeth. We crammed towels
        under the doors to keep from breathing
                dust, hunkering anxiously

while the continent drifted overhead
        in the dark. We banked on the light of day
                to let us voice new lives
                in clear Colorado.

ON MOUNT TIMPANOGOS, 1935

Lodged against the mountain's collarbone
    miles above Provo when I was seven,
        my mother, sister, and I

summered fatherless in a board shack
    whose door we hasped at night
        against the knock-knock of bears.

Eating out of a skillet, we lolled
    naked in aspen-green sunlight,
        felt timid only after dark

in the privy. Mine was the once-a-day task
    of retrieving, from a miserly trickle
        that welled from a seam in the slope,

our few gallons of water. Once the spring filled,
    I'd send a pail racketing along a rope,
        race it down a gravelly path

under the overhead clatter of the pulley
    and dunk it;
        then toil back upward

beneath its sloshing weight of water, vaster
    than you could guess, heaving it,
        consecrated, untouchable.

So words strain upward
    till habit reclaims them
        and they tip into the spillway
        of a lie.

AS I LIVE AND BREATHE AND HAVE MY BEING

Long since pulled down, this house
     breathes in memory
          as redolent of event as dirty

laundry, releasing every odor
     the dwellers inhaled or gave off:
          the smells! Soaps in bathroom

sink or laundry tub, cooling
     grape syrup dripping through doubled cheesecloth
          to settle into jelly, the candied breath

of my young sister nodding half
     out of sleep, the arousal of
          my parents waking and turning

toward one another, Beatrice Tafoya,
     not yet washed, in her maid's bedroom
          downstairs behind the kitchen, the

tang of stale cigarette butts in last
     night's ashtray, the sour vapor
          of undrained glasses of whiskey.

Seven bodies breathed in that house, and I,
     boy of ten, sleeping half in
          half out on a sleeping porch, woke

to the snore and reek of all that
     breathing, and quickly stole down the stairs
          to mount my bicycle and hiss away
          into uncomplicated daylight.

LOVE BETWEEN NOVICES

"Love is so simple," we vowed
    to ourselves, while our nails
        gnawed into our palms.

The body buries its evidence, yet, at the
    rustle of a nightgown,
        its eyes flash.

We spoke after fifty years of resentful
    silence, skin now leathery as
        winter apples, yet the recollection of

the groan of our hapless
    senses still had keenness enough
        to rattle us like hollow trees.

Mismatched yet awkwardly goatish, tender yet
    thickfingered, we clambered up toward
        the lip of a volcano

reciting advisory endearments,
    only to miss our footing
        and slither back into the mere

ashen consolations of the bed. Oh my dear,
    think of my hand, warm on your breast!
        How long we spent hungering for

one another's souls, ignorant that years
    had still to pass before
        either soul would awake
        and arise, arise, arise.

SORRY *(In Memory of Sylvia Plath)*

Lying in his arms I couldn't help
       myself when he kissed me and asked
         why I had done it.

First I told him about my busy time in the city,
       and my return home, and the rebuff.
         Next how I couldn't

sleep, no sleep for weeks—two
       months I told him—without a
         wink. I was surely cracking up.

I had to plan. I could not permit
       myself to become a burden to
         Mother. He kissed me again.

I told him about the swim, far out, but
       I couldn't get tired enough. And about
         the razor I couldn't press deep.

About the pills I stole from Mother and added my own
       and wrote the note and crawled
         under the porch and slept at last.

When I woke up my cheek was full of maggots.
       In the hospital they broke my head
         with lightning bolts. Everyone was so *kind.*

Then I felt his body chill. He actually
       felt sorry for me. That bastard.
         Sorry! I could claw him.
         He understood nothing.

RING OF RINGS

Brilliant token, the gold
        strap or sparkler
                brightening a single finger

on her hand proclaims
        that the cattle have been
                conveyed, the bride-price

forked over: the wearer on the street, flicking
        her finger, exhibits
                all those transactions.

Her intimacies, silently
        exulting at the entrance
                of a congenial phallus,

welcome the newcomer to
        their dedicated spaces. Tent-stays
                stretched, the halyards made fast

for grand openings, one
        flap akimbo, the egg
                readies itself. In public

her proud face says nothing, but
        the light shining from her brandished
                ring finger says: *Do not kiss*

this sweet knuckle.
        It is spoken for, may not
                be shared. I have
                been singled out.

YOU

From beyond the borders of memory, you seemed to
    gaze, to unfold, clothe me,
        lift me. I was held, washed,

fed. On unsprung legs I swayed and
    tottered. Your smile urged me into
        walking. Your words urged me out

into words. Your scowl stunned and guarded me. You taught,
    scolded, attended. *And now, you vanish.*
        What dark seas must I canvass to

undrown you? How far have you drifted,
    castaway? I yearn
        across pathless waterlands for

a whiff of your sour fragrance, a waft
    of dimpled arms, the flick and murmur of
        your speaking, the groan of your soft song,

the pursed kisses of your mouth.
    Who could have thought you would ever so
        immoderately disappear? Or imagine

that, no matter how hard I haul
    on the ligaments of our fateful
        connection, you

could never possibly return,
    never respond, never
        speak, never
        know me?

SEASIDE SUMMER QUARRY

While a waterlily shivers and
    shrugs its shadow over
        a green platter of leaf,

two water striders caper across
    their liquid runway to climb
        the next lilypad,

surmounting a dark-brown tea-steeped
    dangerous depth
        of water.

Sentried by sabers of iris,
    bared granite rocks
        jut up

from soft starry beds of
    emerald moss, their harsh hide
        hairy with gray

and green lichens. The dull leaves
    of past seasons lie low
        in crevices. From the high sky

gold strands of sunlight thread
    through the hemlocks.
        Over my shoulder, fishboat diesels

thrum their dark discord
    against the snarl of a
        small plane, while,

flap! and crack! in a freshening
        breeze, sloop-sails
                make good their getaway.

Rapt here in the quarry, under a wide
        straw hat, you
                sit still and with a pen

not yet quite released
        into perfect freedom,
                endeavor to fix

upon your sheet of paper
        the same stolen abstractions
                I have just lost
                from mine.

II

Nor Age, But . . .

BEST FRIEND

Memory, till now, has kept inviting
     new printings as often as
          it reads out old ones. What a huge

noise it makes! Songs, poems, postures, a slice
     of an opera, a warm mouthful of potato
          pizza, a sexy occurrence

on a couch in Kansas, the chalky gesture of
     a classroom teacher, the stench of a faraway
          pig farm: I never need ask it

a favor. It lets me into adjoining lives
     by their back doors, recovering nothing
          I have ever been indifferent to,

even acts omitted (the chap-lipped freckled girl
     unkissed, my stinking enemy set scot-free).
          Five senses should suffice, but memory

lends me a way of embracing them all.
     Without it I'd be a traffic-jam of
          sensations; only with its help may I revisit

myself. Kinetically selective, it guides me
     into the *Heiliger Dankgesang,* Sappho's ode,
          the flavor of Blatz, the color

of a mountain bluebird, the lost face
     of my mother. Memory cherishes
          every self it has ever cared for.
          Ghastly friend! Don't let me drown.

PHANTOM PAIN

1. Surgery: Morphine

No pain at all, but void. Oh, for more pain!
I yearn to wrap you in my arms, although
I can reach out to nothing touchable.
Embodiments of you have brushed against me
in every city. Everybody's body
concealed within your body reaches out
to seize the Me who relishes the You.

2. Hallucination: Percocet

I awoke in the dark of winter when your voice
reached out to me from a thousand miles away,
as though the sound, sent, were still arriving, and
I could anticipate its touch upon
my naked bedwarm body, half northerly
and half remote, from among the palms and beaches.
So did I wrap you in gossamer,
tender as music, warm as a gift, protecting you
from heat, from cold, from everything but pleasure.

3. Convalescence: Codeine

Tongue, stretch to your roots. Jaws, unclasp
to disengage the great nerve of the neck.
Eyes, roll, squeeze shut. Hips, rise, rotate.
Arms, fling wide and gather in embrace
armfuls of air, of sound, of tone.
Music! Let us be true to one another.
False quantities, dig up, scuttle away

down spine, out feet. Shake off weight, underscore
entanglements, outworn and bashful,
weary words, withered sensations.

4. Recovery: Distant Effects

The wires don't touch—or if they do, they sputter
and suddenly—no flash—electrocute:
distant effects. These clumsy fingers stutter
while fumbling with the buttons of my suit.
Flusters of ache transform the knees to butter
evoking toe of frog or eye of newt.
Back into bed. The names of lovers flutter
like notes that hurry through a hollow flute.
Who calls this healing? Leave it to the gods
to prop our failing bodies in a place
where we'll investigate the false position
we never happened to hold. Now, against the odds,
arrive the scent of love, the darling face
to rescue everything, the sweet physician.

LITTLE DEATH

I escaped, spinning off
      to heaven knows what
            hideaway, eluding

control, threatening to
      relinquish: to end up
            bland, inert.

Without intake how should I not
      become my own dull
            monument, lie

immobile, cold as winter dirt, in-
      communicado? Unless I
            exert effort

my presence could harden into
      dead stone. Yet I must and will
            continue. Chest

heaves. Limbs lengthen. Head
      hums with vestiges of
            memory that pick up the scent

of desire. Body starts
      breathing. Listen!
            Bloodstream thumps

once more, tingling. Before
      I can so much as stir,
         my hair
           resumes growing.

MY FATHER'S HUNDREDTH BIRTHDAY

Not only the moon face, scarlet
    with coughing, and the miracle voice
        (as resonant as Swansea Dylan's), but

his very smell, sweet as copra,
    tiptoes down to me now over the
        leaky decades.

He bled away at seventy-one yet still
    vibrates in every word of every
        poem I ever heard him remember

as vocally as the heart that clanged within him.
    His eyes widened, his vowels dripped
        with honey, his consonants

prickled and hissed (in English, which
    "among living tongues the Muse most delights to honour")
        in traversing the processions of poetry.

He spoke each strophe for its gesture, how it
    welcomed ceremony, tiff, procreation,
        worship, pain, instigation, or

death. He preached, wheedled,
    ranted, exulted, or whimpered, never
        cushioning any poem with mittened hands

as a conundrum, or as "text." He
    savaged adversaries with the blast of his voice
        yet plumbed the marrow of poetry as tenderly
        as if a darling had crept into his arms.

For Edward Davison, July 28, 1998

21

THE RITUALS

A twig tapped on
    a plate, a spoon
        clinked on a cup,

a late-afternoon robin
    let fly his half-hearted
        evening tirade as I

sat beneath the flicking leather
    leaves of the beech tree,
        and the supple grass of the meadow

fanned before the push of evening air
    like boozy sweat
        trickling over the thin surfaces

of my chest. Now that another
    day's die is cast, have I
        any choice but to

shrug away from the gathering convention
    of mosquitoes into the hospitable
        enclave of the house, gulp

from a glass, make ready
    to macerate a little
        parsley, shove some

rice in a circle in a skillet, think
    about what to think about while I eat it, and
        shift to the dark rituals of
        staying alive till morning?

LOSING IT

The scent of memory drifts down
        in gusts from the hills of the past.
                The book I stowed yesterday

has been swallowed up. The nickname
        I knew as well as my own
                has absolutely decamped

though I could have sworn it would come back to me.
        Lips parted eagerly, I've found
                myself retaining very little

memory of remembering. I've burst into
        sudden fits of lust with
                no known precedent.

Some say age shrinks perception. My senses
        run riot, scampering
                happily in and out of tune,

though no doubt the turnstiles
        will shortly jam. At this stage
                I'm hovering half in and half out

of my mind, one foot squelching in a juicy
        swamp of invention, the other
                jammed in hardening concrete.

Hovering, squinty, I crouch like
        a disorderly ancient of days
                setting his warped measure
                to the earth.

ACCUSTOMED TO EXISTENCE

He finally spoke up, without smiling
    (why should he smile?) during dessert at the club,
        announcing news of

threatening ailments and loose
    cargoes. Symptoms. Prognoses.
        He recounted them without

frown, sweat, or hyperventilation: if the
    cancer didn't bloom, the
        coronary artery might pop, or

the aneurysm fizzle into
    the brain, and the red curtain
        fall.

No smiling matter, though the doctors
    might offer options
        later, doing their

duty, driven to blunt answers.
    What did finding a solution matter
        to him now, or even to

his wife? As well advise a man who
    is accustomed to existence to stop
        breathing until and unless

he can certify where his next breath is coming from!
    Which of us would dare tell him to
        stop living merely because
        he was going to die?

TWO PERPLEXITIES

1. *Forgetting Names*

Sure I lose track. At my age
    handles don't help
        any more than files do. Or Organizers.

Every face is new. Noises
    speak out of each voice
        intoned by the slopes of its teeth, guided

by the hapless shrug of its gestures.
        Cruikshank. Carpenter. Rosenberg. Why not
        Bentleg? Woodworker? Rosy Hill?

Don't paint me dumb pictures, tell me about *you.*
    Unless you insist on being tucked
        into a dynasty, like

Louis the Fat or Eva Gabor, give me a name that fits you.
    That-sidewise-smile? Husky-
        voice? Grimace-of-distaste? I'd know you

anywhere. Better label yourself Frances Glum or Antoine
    Whinny than keep on murmuring monikers (like
        Felix Rohatyn,

Jean Smith, Egregio Galante) that could get stuck
    on anybody. The fact is,
        names don't count. They'll

never match the Johnny-Jump-Up of
    your face. Me, I'm superstitious. I dub thee Nemo,
        Nameless, Distinguished. Holy
        Entity that needs no name.

2. *What Ails You*

"Germs" used to take the fall, but latterly
      we blame our food first, turning next
            to the Relaxation Response.

Cause, effect, who knows? Something's amiss:
      a tearing ache in the intercostal
            connections, a nagging

tugging at the thigh, a searing
      implosion at play
            in the lower intestine . . . Last Tuesday

I located a thickening in the soles of my feet.
      My eyes grow dim. My hearing's inconstant.
            No explanation suffices, certainly not

the ingenuities of my medical record
      and its referrals, which keep tracking
            ills without nabbing them.

We have somehow failed
      in the mighty task of Wellness. No doubt
            we're all lax about diet, disregard

exercise, and persist in deplorably
      judgmental attitudes, but
            let's face facts:

if you have awakened today
      and you're over sixty
            and you don't hurt anywhere
            you must be dead.

STEEP

The path is steepening. It must be mine.
        The nostrils flare at each familiar scent.
Legs, will you carry me past timberline?

Should I have taken steepness for a sign
        to stigmatize the journey that I went?
This path is steepening: it must be mine.

My parents crooned and kissed, an intertwine
        whose love grew limp despite their best intent.
Legs, will you carry me past timberline?

Other old stories toe the party line:
        "The senses rule the journey." "I was lent
this path." "It's steepening? It must be mine."

With splintered footholds, ice that chills the spine,
        lifting's the thing, not fault or accident.
Legs, will you carry me past timberline,

limping, exhausted, nearing the confine
        where breathing is the ultimate event?
This path is steepening. It must be mine.
Legs, will you carry me past timberline?

III

An After Dinner's Sleep . . .

THESE DAYS

Days when it's easy, the water
      seems wonderfully clear, not a
            chance of drowning. Objects

appear so close that you need only
      reach down for them into coolness
            until the word offers up:

as though you could shape thought with
      your thumb. Around you the air
            dissolves into names for itself.

The noise of the waves tearing
      the shore apart blooms like
            French horns. The taste

of the self is sweet. These days
      it's easy to forget how
            stubborn silence can be, how

rapidly glibness drains the mind of every
      nutrient, what fanatic reinforcements
            the armies of emptiness insist on bringing forward.

These days every choice is clear, every
      location opens at a touch to
            yield its necessary

drop of honey, every word glows
      with exactly the wanted
            intensity of
            tilt.

PRAYER TO THE VERB

Fingering language for a pulse
       that, with a sprinkle
           of luck added,

might entice feeling from its shelter,
       I wait out your awakening. You're
           not to be waylaid, are you,

no chance of that? Your breathing
       crouches expectantly in the silence
           of the entrance to the mouth

(serving also as exit): a rough tunnel
       along which energy noses out
           and shrinks back,

protecting within dubious straits
       the actual world the creature
           entertains

within itself, the
       sanctity of its creation.
           I pray that you, blessèd verb,

may deploy beyond us, that my hand,
       stretching across
           the graveyard of the inanimate

with your quickening touch,
       may encounter more
           than the mere crust of
           whatever throbbed there.

GETTING OVER ROBERT FROST

All those evenings cradled in the sway
  of the old man's gnarled hands
    gently chopping the air

woke my nostrils to the fragrance of
  my mind, eased out
    the frequencies my ears could reach.

Such an influence seeps in and stays.
  I'm thankful
    for his friendship, as I'm indebted to my

genes—though it's taken years to comprehend
  that a great poet is only a great
    poet: neither a father nor a force

of generation. I was born entitled to
  the liberty of breathing easy, but I had to learn
    the trick of not trusting a line

unless it flickered with
  my own odor, the taste of
    myself. And then I got over him,

welcoming the little victories of
  waking up, learning that not all harmonies
    need to be prodded or bent

to take on tragic overtones, that
  music need not always express
    regret at having
    disappointed someone.

GLITTERING TROUT

Throbbing back through
      the insistent years whose currents
            of sensation have thrashed

over me, my heart startles, yet now
      I yearn more wildly than ever. Finally
            perhaps I've hushed the lispings

of childhood: dew on a dry morning,
      the sweet reek of hay, the whole-mouth
            flavor of milk.

Memories supply later scenarios, chromatic
      melodies: a woman throwing open, with a smile,
            her gown and settling down like a naked moth

over me. A snowbank where
      my flushed snowsuited little sister
            wriggles laughing in the cold. The savor

and kick of a still-smoking army rifle.
      The rueful eyes, cornflower blue,
            of my dead wife, smiling. The dull refusal

of a keyboard as it withholds the true pitch or the just
      word. The fierce ache of
            fury at being opposed.

Finally I float on the surface of my remembered
      millpond. My senses stoop
            to catch poems without bait,
            glittering trout.

VILLA DEI PINI

The wind combs the pines, trying out
       every needle with its soft
              fingers. Under the trees

two old retrievers, one mouthing half
       a tennis ball, lollop their daily
              inspection of the cliffside:

a whiff here for a spiderplant, a pause
       there at a yucca, a full stop
              to hunch a turd into the precise center of

the footpath. Inside the house, dishes clatter, beds
       are being tucked up, residents arm with sweaters
              for a cool morning of brainwork, while

through the tilted cliff that holds up the house,
       trains tunnel and scream, Genoa
              to La Spezia. Above

the hissing shore, where reefs
       interrupt the cobalt sea with
              foaming intervention,

neutral gulls, carrying a gray blot
       behind each ear, sideslip and wail
              over the long-trafficked

water. Here pirates seized slaves, and
       crusaders set sail
              to confirm their faith
              by the massacre of infidels.

PATHWAY

Hogarth named it "the line of beauty."
    As it launches into meadow
        the path follows the sinuous median

of the human female, a curve
    that most intimately states our
        position: no straight stretches, no

facile outcomes, no solutions whatever.
    It emerges from our lawn,
        ascends a slight slope between outcrops,

declines through a tangle of clover and vetch
    toward its low point, mucky in season.
        It lifts to engage a plantation

of poison ivy and plunges on into
    the shade of pine, pin-oak, and sassafras.
        Roots jut up underfoot through moss until

the path sallies out into sunlight:
    a level field, grassy, where
        horses have trodden a ring,

leaving behind *walk, trot,* and *canter*
    to echo into the air and freeze
        into the soil. You, with your

safely shod toes, which way now?
    Skirmish into the unplucked forest? Or
        fall back upon the pillowed house
        by the way you came?

UNDER THE LANGUAGE SEA

Through the velvet silence
      that sustains me, nouns
            dart, their gills pulsing

like adjectives, their fins
      delivering them up
            like verbs. I can almost

hear oxygen trickle through
      their tiny capillaries, sifted
            from the liquor of the sea,

almost predict how and when
      immanent electricity will
            fire them with blue-green light.

They ease around me, but after
      lingering awhile they'll pass on their way,
            tails thrashing,

tiny currents settling at their backs into
      usual darkness. Between visits I'll
            simply hold myself

attentive, maintaining life afloat
      among seizures and checkbooks, asphalt
            and mailmen, unbreathing

beneath the glittering sea-surface,
      insentient as a black
            sea-cucumber
            or inching starfish.

A HISTORY OF READING

1. The Body

Breezes whorled and plinked bare arms.
The body squirmed, trilled back in echo.
Illiterate in the face of sensation,
nature and human breathed in a single system—
so intricately attached an animal!
Experience lay at hand, in touch, splayed open,
dedicated in intercourse, in sleep, in breathing.

2. The Page

Thousands of years later the beast had learned
somehow to carry, on a mere leaf,
the memory he need no longer try to remember.
When he revisited his runes he could recapture
the touch of the breeze, the sough of the prayers,
the trill of the stories. Once he learned to
visualize those by hefting the mere weight of the leaf,
he might unstore his treasuries again.

3. The Book

Having carried all those leaves as reminders,
he could fasten them into a sheaf to retain
shifting breezes, hot prayers, linked stories
to save for perusal or delivery to others.
Whenever he chose not to be alone,
he could open up that supply and enter.
The leaves would carry him away in any direction
by means of precise ranks and files.

4. The Library

What if the store desired
should stand far off
or loom very large? Could not some device
convey all the memories of the world,
quick march, to the top of a shining table,
breezes, prayers, stories
all instantly to hand,
plucked without mediation
out of the vast inventory without
fingering even a leaf?
Might we, seated, feel the faint breeze,
hear the murmured prayer,
follow the pale gleam of the story?

5. The Circuit

It has happened. Each time
I stroke a key it diverts me
to circuits that forward the quick march
to other circuits, rescinding the chance of choices.
By the time I arrive at
the location of the leaf of my prayer,
the yearning has been hemmed in.
I cannot recognize it as mine,
for it has been altered by
the mediating that hedges its spaces.

6. The Outcome

Yes, the message survives, but
the impulse has faded.
A faint white signal replicates
cool breeze, green leaf,

rich store, ordered march,
clarified, precise.
Mediated. Meditated. Ruled.
A victory parade of lies.

IV

Dreaming of . . .

FARMER & WIFE

sleep a lot, winters (less so
        as springtime shoves daylight toward
            its limits, and birdly

orchestras intensify dawn's clamor).
        Weeding, watering, milking, and emergency
            adjustments to fencewire and balers

flicker through our blinkered nights.
        Dark seasons stifle us, just as enlarged daylight
            will insist that we recalculate our chances.

Our children, near grown, have been swaying to
        distant music, flagellations of desire
            manipulated by "world-famous talent agents."

Neighbors are constrained to trade up, selling out
        to the enticements of Real Estate
            and their intensifying need for

quick-acting contraptions. The black soil of
        our acreage drinks deeper and deeper from
            poisoned sources.

Although our harvests blandly persist, yielding
        sweet forage as well as stubborn
            burdock, in our winter sleep

we can hear the future
        inching up nightly
            into its own, into the sure
            day of our permanent exile.

FOR LACK OF A TREATY

They're not put out, the storks
    and pelicans, by hourly flights
        of reconnaissance aircraft

howling and buzzing the great marsh
    beneath the Golan. Feathery
        priorities stir up

a raucous congress of migrants in their daily
    debate under the Heights.
        For thirty years this

migratory flyway has served its trustees
    as flyover country. Competing
        claims are filed by

ornithologists with 'scopes and glasses
    tiptoeing tensely along
        planks of boardwalk to

focus on egret and teal, wagtail and
    kingfisher. All the while overhead
        jets and 'copters froth

and snarl at the Syrians,
    proclaiming sovereign rights in
        these groves of

papyrus, these shrubs and
    mangroves that have cradled
        a hundred thousand generations
        of birds.

RUFFED GROUSE

The buds let fly a pungent spring flavor,
      and the sunlight fanned across
            the bare ground for unperching.

Restlessness crept in, a necklace
      around the male's long neck, below where
            his beak would open to sing,

if he were the kind to sing. His
      back gathered itself to lengthen and
            widen. He needed more room now

and soon found it in a clearing he had been
      keeping his eye on, with a
            hollow log planted at one edge.

Now he had to wait only a day or two
      until something in the air called, *Time!*
            before he'd start to grow. His clawed toes prepared to

tick on the leaves, his strut to shorten. His
      hidden shoulders would soon begin their
            burgeoning, beyond wings, into the

great hissing ruff. The tail would stiffen, and within
      his chest new lungs would at last open. Now
            his pace would march him

strut by strut toward the hidden music, to
      mount the hollow log, shuffle
            his feathered feet, and *drum drum drum*
            drum drum till the whole forest shuddered.

TWO SNAPPING TURTLES

1. June Clutch

Lengthening days enlightened me
      among the algae. Now they could not
            grow longer: my year was full.

Land called me to the harsh bank, to crush
      the dry leaves from last year's short days.
            Up the bluff, climbed, fell,

climbed, all night upward, crawling,
      till day exposed me, rapt and arrived
            at the Sand Place, sky open.

Dawn reddened as I scraped my spot
      near my sisters' laying grounds,
            scratched deep and with absolute

effort planted what I had,
      spasm after spasm, as the light came up. I
            pressed my eggs down into the warm soil.

I expelled more of me and more
      until I was empty and it was done. *Oh, done.*
            Rest soon. I managed to edge

out of the high sun toward
      deep shade, stride upon stride, hauling
            my heavy hardness to the bluff,

tumbled over the edge, gratefully down, and tramped
      across the road, past the dry leaves,
            to the dark lapping edge of the
            welcome and eternal water.

2. September Hatch

I woke to the dark
    slowly long since
        while forces rolled far

off above me. I grew. Other
    hatchlings nestled at my side. Earth
        turned summer-hot, dryer,

settling into cool. Silence
    helped nourish me into completion.
        I found I could stir

head, limbs if only
    the earth would permit passage.
        At last it opened. The

equable sky guttered above.
    My companions—my kin—released from
        dark soil stirred

beside me then crept, tottered upward
    out of confinement trudging along
        a familiar precipitous

path toward the aim of home,
    doom, echoing
        motherland, down beyond

the unfamiliarity of light
    toward the pole
        of it all toward
        the dark welcoming water.

TO A TAME PLANT

Leathery, embossed, you curl under
    yourself like a closing fist,
        moisture summoned within you

from a source root-deep,
    far distant, somewhere
        earthward. You send up

payments to the sun so that
    light may configure all
        your energies into what

nourishes your stout stalk, your
    scalloped contours, your rootbound
        hoof crammed in its pot!

You press your thrust upward
    toward a ceiling under which no
        jungle floor sustains you, where

no howler monkey or scream of
    toucan echoes beneath the canopy,
        where you entertain no

companion from your own
    habitat but stand neatly among
        ranked shelves of obedient citizens

sheltered under glass,
    warmed by furnace heat supplied
        by the long-ago decay of
        your fellow flora.

WALKING THROUGH THE BIG DIG

Foot follows foot, splat splat on the unsettled
      basic brick of Boston's teetering
          unsteady sidewalks,

harder than ever to follow these days, wilfully
      shifting azimuth and intention: last week
          one way, this week another. Eternal

vigilance is required. Example: the cold ruby eye
      of a street pigeon, looking up while
          sorting out a gutter spill of unpopped popcorn.

He scuttles to escape my splat-splat. Next I have to
      shrink back to avoid clashing
          with the groans of a tenwheeled

dumptruck of gravel and muck, closely chased by
      a screeching dumptruck of empty. Splat splat.
          A minyan of hardhats assembles where

a newly unearthed well of yellow water
      nibbles at a deep trench. Before a
          tipsy streetlight I'm halted,

baffled by the rubbery black approach
      of a funeral cortege. I have no choice now but
          to behave. Credit my Colorado

upbringing: as the hearse passes, clap hat in hand,
      cover the heart with it.
          Stand at attention.
          Pay respect.

LIKE NO OTHER

As I followed my road
            the atmosphere altered
                        into a susurrus under the pines

and took shape in the lightfoot
            lope of a rapt fox
                        a red and ragged vixen

absorbed in her intentions
            taking no notice that
                        I was about to cross

her path. Closing fast
            catlike or rather foxlike
                        in concentration she

pursued a faint
            trail across the road
                        under a fallen tree

toward the kits in her lair
            coming from the lake
                        her belly full of water

nose half lowered
            to where
                        deer showed. The ground

reeked with the odors
            of forest traffic
                        as her track led
                        away into her woods.

FALLING WATER

Wherever it commences perhaps as random
      raindrop tapping on a leaf and tumbling
            into a tea-stained mosscup

it helplessly inquires after
      lower levels whether seeping
            darkly through silt

and marl to enlarge an imprisoned
      aquifer shortcut or taking its chances to trickle
            out through a slit of clay to join its first

brook and amble off into the yielding
      soft-shouldered marsh past fat roots of
            lilies to linger among the slick fronds

of algae paddled by ducks pierced by
      pickerel to hurry itself and whisk
            into the outlet that will boil it

along a streambed of gravel toward another
      stairstep of idleness the lax
            lake spritzed with yawning sun

there to seek a breach to tip and hurtle
      into torrent and the great meander
            that will sweep it out and away

to empty into the broad salt
      sleep that will cradle it until
            the sun siphons it again
            to knit into more rain.

V

. . . Both

BREATHING ROOM

Though they rise upon
        a column of the breath, poems rarely
                evoke the ulcerated saints who long ago

crouched on pillars in the desert. The poem
        hovers distracted above its
                fastness yet remains

attentive to events. Tick
        of sand-grains. Gleam of wet blood
                from the distant beak of a

wheeling vulture. Softness of
        a cloud unveiling the moon.
                Holding the poem's breath,

the planet turns, transmitting tremors
        along its sundial shaft
                to the capital where, stranded

but alert, intelligence agencies perceive
        the spicy cooling scents
                of night, eavesdrop on

desert mice, accept promptings from
        every source: the legend of
                Atlas who shouldered the world,

the memory of fallen forests, the parched
        indelible tiretracks of Land Rovers,
                the radiant clamor of noonday, the
                icy silence of the stars.

A BALLAD

He taught her what he knew,
    his craft with animals,
        his way with nightmares.

She swallowed each draught,
    thirsting for
        more, more, more,

not only the dissolved
    secrets of poetry, but
        to sate every hunger.

He took pride in his teachings:
    he beamed to see his wife
        emerge dripping, newborn,

a created self. Yet as she strode
    her path
        she stumbled over old

specters that slipped their
    leashes. She nosed,
        anxious for outcome,

along the brow of a seaside
    bluff, cried for a kiss of
        the black shoe of

her primal abuser, for
    the cakecrumb comfort of her
        cooing mother, for

the titty appetites of children.
   Her nightmares blossomed into
     deeprooted elms:

her ailing neighbor withered;
   stumplegged amputees
     crowded the beach,

limping. And on a May morning
   another woman
     sidled into the ripe garden,

ready to strip off her own
   nightmare. The poet's
     dream catcher

snatched at her, hypnotizing
   those hollow dark eyes.
     He boomed back

at this woman from the rim
   of his own
     cultivated nightmare.

Suddenly more nightmares
   scuttled out of hiding into every
     cranny of the countryside

Sobbing, snarling, snatching
   her children away from the
     nimbus of their father,

the wife yearned for a distant city,
   pressed two small heads
     against her milky breasts,

abandoning beehive and graveyard
  for the cold crowds of
    London. Woe

weighed upon the wife, harsh
  as a glacier. She kept her vigil
    while the moon crackled. At last

on one frozen morning
  she lay breathless and congealed. Two
    orphans whimpered for milk.

Their father huddled
  back under thatch together
    with the two children and

the other woman's cattle-car of
  nightmares. They clustered for warmth
    and in time nursed

a third child, begotten out
  of the tangle. The
    nightmare thickened

and weighed. This woman,
  lying alone on the wife's mattress,
    gave ear to the chorus

of horrors
  as they scrambled back from
    the immigrant dark. She

swept herself
  and her wide-eyed child
    out into the gassy forever.

Dumbstruck, the twice-wounded
        shaman, the wifeless father,
                librarian of nightmares,

crouched in the dark
        of a widower's hutch,
                encircled by the curses

of his two dead women,
        rattled by the hungers
                of his two live children.

Haunted by a heap of
        the wife's poems
                that beckoned, shuddered, and

squirmed on the kitchen table,
        he would roam restless,
                a gaunt crow

cawing at hints and invitations,
        fragments of dreams,
                all the while

lugging over his shoulder the
        hive of growling bees
                that his wife had

willed him to care for.
        The queen-bee's hum
                broadened into a roar,

honey crystallizing
        into amber gemstone.
                A chorus of women

shrieked at the poet, and
       his destiny shrank back.
              At long last it returned, in

the hunky shape of
       advancing death. The
          curator of

nightmares saddled up
       to escape,
           lashing his mounts,

borrowing every nag
       the livery of past poetry
          could lend him:

the wrenching shape-shifts of Ovid,
       the ferocities of Racine,
          the murderous rapture

of justice-maddened Aeschylus.
       Only now could he disclose
          his own wounds, light up

the dark runes his wife
       had left to hiss
          in her wake. He turned

about and stared
       at her ghost,
          at her frozen face,

shriving himself with the nightmares
       that had long ago gruntled them
          into the same bed.

He chewed his lip for
        the cruelties
                they had inflicted on

one another. Finally, before he died,
        those two caught their breath
                together again. Her poems still

shrug like an osprey alone
        in its sky, riding
                a shriek of American pain,

while his murk
        rumbles through the
                battle-scarred body

of English poetry,
        clenching a bruised
                fist. The lovers

lie apart in
        immortal mismarriage,
                deafened by pangs of

need unlistened to,
        bright scar of rage,
                the last word spoken.

THE LEVEL PATH

Descend here along a shower of
    shallow steps past the potting shed with
        its half-rotted ironbound door

to reach the level path. It winds
    northward, high hat, girdling
        the waist of a limestone cliff

beyond earshot of the clamorous village below. The
    squeezed access bears us vaguely along
        shifting digressions of the compass, past

eye-level seductions of violet, periwinkle, primrose, and petals
    like lisping yellow butterflies. Naked limbs
        of beech, haggard liftings of pine,

a hairy upthrust of cedar beside a
    curving stone bench, all hint at eruptions
        into Eros. Yet another seat displays

a cushion of undisturbed luxuriant moss around its clefts and
    edges. Thick harsh leaves
        of holly, ivy, even of palmetto

thrust up, pathside, between tender new petals,
    while other friendly shrubs reach down
        from overhead to fondle our faces.

There is no escape from the dreadful beauty of
    this narrow path. It leads nowhere
        except to itself and
        the black water below.

NO ESCAPE

No, not yet, move nothing until
    you have filled yourself with
        intention, or

your act will freeze, immutable, and
    your thought will have aborted
        into misshapen stumbling.

We stammer in the effort to speak, lurch
    out of a passion to walk, slump
        in lieu of sitting; yet,

within, awareness may reach toward
    an attainable state in which
        we seek to direct our selves

as a rider guides the most accomplished of
    horses, crupper gathering, hooves
        pattering, neck yearning toward

heaven, the supple trunk conveying
    itself over the earth without
        anticipation or effort.

This is the ascent into the self,
    encountering possibility just as it
        flowers into the actual.

We attain fulfilment only if we carry
    the breath of the world
        without surrender
        or escape.

ACKNOWLEDGMENTS

Earlier versions of these poems were first published elsewhere as follows:

The Atlantic Monthly: "Best Friend," "Falling Water," "Like No Other,"
     "No Escape," "On Mount Timpanogos, 1935," "These Days," "You"
Boston Globe: "Walking Through the Big Dig"
Country Journal: "Pathway"
DoubleTake: "Confederates," "Farmer & Wife"
Five Points: "Accustomed to Existence," "Losing It," "Phantom Pain,"
     "The Rituals," "Villa dei Pini"
The Georgia Review: "My Father's Hundredth Birthday"
Michigan Quarterly Review: "A History of Reading," "Prayer to the Verb"
The Nation: "Breathing Room"
The New Republic: "Under the Language Sea"
Orion: "Two Snapping Turtles"
The Paris Review: "Little Death"
Partisan Review: "Seaside Summer Quarry"
Poetry: "What Ails You"
Stand: "Ruffed Grouse," "The Level Path"
The Yale Review: "Glittering Trout"

The New Breadloaf Anthology of Contemporary American Poetry:
     "On Mount Timpanogos, 1935," "Little Death," "Falling Water"
The Poetry of New England: "Falling Water," "Like No Other"

A NOTE ON THE TYPE

The text of this book was set in Simoncini Garamond, a modern version by Francesco Simoncini of the type attributed to the famous Parisian type cutter Claude Garamond (ca. 1480–1561). Garamond was a pupil of Geoffroy Tory and is believed to have based his letters on the Venetian models, although he introduced a number of important differences, and it is to him we owe the letter that we know as old-style. He gave to his letters a certain elegance and a feeling of movement that won for their creator an immediate reputation and the patronage of Francis I of France.

Composed by NK Graphics, Keene, New Hampshire
Printed and bound by Edwards Brothers, Inc., Ann Arbor, Michigan
Designed by Dorothy S. Baker